CW00802013

Mixology Cocktails

The best recipes of the most famous cocktails with tips and tricks of the best bartenders in the world

Fuzz Chris

Copyright © 2021 *Fuzz Chris*

All rights reserved.

Table of content

© Copyright 2021 by Fuzz Chris - All rights reserved.

The following Book is reproduced below with the goal of providing information that is as accurate and reliable as possible. Regardless, purchasing this Book can be seen as consent to the fact that both the publisher and the author of this book are in no way experts on the topics discussed within and that any recommendations or suggestions that are made herein are for entertainment purposes only. Professionals should be consulted as needed prior to undertaking any of the action endorsed herein. This declaration is deemed fair and valid by both the American Bar Association and the Committee of Publishers Association and is legally binding throughout the United States. Furthermore, the transmission, duplication, or reproduction of any of the following work including specific information will be considered an illegal act irrespective of if it is done electronically or in print. This extends to creating a secondary or tertiary copy of the work or a recorded copy and is only allowed with the express written consent from the Publisher. All additional right reserved. The information in the following pages is broadly considered a truthful and accurate account of facts and as such, any inattention, use, or misuse of the information in question by the reader will render any resulting actions solely under their purview. There are no scenarios in which the publisher or the original author of this work can be in any fashion deemed liable for any hardship or damages that may befall them after undertaking information described herein. Additionally, the information in the following pages is intended only for informational purposes and should thus be thought of as universal. As befitting its nature, it is presented without assurance regarding its prolonged validity or interim quality. Trademarks that are mentioned are done without written consent and can in no way be considered an endorsement from the trademark holder.

Tips and tricks

How can you resist the opportunity to craft a tasty cocktail? Learning how to mix great drinks is fun and it is not difficult. If you're looking to dive deeper into the world of the bar—whether at home or as a pro—then a crash course in bartending is just what you need. With a few basic tools and a handful of tips and tricks, your next drinks can be better than any you've made before.

Anyone Can Make Great Cocktails

One of the greatest myths about cocktails is that they're difficult to make and you might even be asking yourself if it's worth it. Is making a pizza from scratch worth the time? Absolutely! All of the joy and excitement you get out of cooking can be found in the bar as well—even if that bar is in your kitchen.Think of the flavor combinations you can create and new drinks you can explore.Picture the look on your friends' faces when you whip out your cocktail shaker.Imagine how much money you'll save when you can replace those $12 martinis at the bar.There are serious benefits to learning a few bartending skills and you'll have a ton of fun at the same time. Booze, fruit, maybe a little chocolate, how can you say "no" to that?

Mixing a great drink has a certain satisfaction to it as well, it's an accomplishment to be proud of and a skill set that you can share with others. Don't keep it to yourself, invite some friends over and enjoy the process together.

1. Seamstress Irish Coffee

INGREDIENTS

DIRECTIONS

- 1 3/4 ounces Slane Irish Whiskey
- 1/2 ounce Demerara simple syrup (2 to 1, sugar to water)
- 2 1/2 ounces hot coffee
- 1 ounce cream float (recipe follows)

In a heatproof Georgian glass, add Slane Irish Whiskey, Demerara simple syrup and coffee.

Leave room at the top for the heavy cream.

Stir gently.

Float a thin layer of cream on top.

Garnish with a healthy grating of fresh cinnamon.

2. Aviation Cocktail

INGREDIENTS

DIRECTIONS

- 1½ ounce gin
- ½ to ¾ ounce Maraschino liqueur
- ¾ ounce fresh lemon juice
- ¼ ounce crème de violette
- ¼ ounce simple syrup

Combine all ingredients in a cocktail shaker and fill with ice.
Shake well, then double-strain into a chilled coupe.

3. Piña Colada

INGREDIENTS

- 2 oz White Rum
- 2 oz Coconut Cream
- 2 oz Pineapple Juice
- Pineapple leaf

DIRECTIONS

Combine all ingredients, except pineapple leaf, in shaker.
Add ice to fill.
Shake vigorously, until shaker is frosted over.
Fill hurricane glass with crushed ice.
Strain cocktail into glass.
Garnish with pineapple leaf and enjoy.

4. Strawberry Bellini

INGREDIENTS

DIRECTIONS

2 fresh strawberries
¼ ounce lemon juice
1 teaspoon sugar
3 ounces Prosecco

Blend strawberries with sugar and a touch of lemon juice
Pour puree into a coupe or Champagne flute
Top with Prosecco
Garnish with additional strawberry

5. Brandy Crusta

INGREDIENTS

DIRECTIONS

1 ½ oz Brandy
½ oz Maraschino Liqueur
¾ oz Triple Sec
¾ oz Lemon
1 dash Angostura
1 dash Peychaud's

Combine all ingredients in a wine glass.
Add crushed ice.
Garnish with large lemon twist and enjoy.

6. Mandarin Bramble

INGREDIENTS

DIRECTIONS

2 ounces white rum
2 ounces fresh-squeezed mandarin juice
1 ounce lemon juice
1 ounce pomegranate syrup, such as Monin.

Combine rum, mandarin juice, and lemon juice in a cocktail shaker with ice.
Shake to chill and combine.
Strain ingredients into a large cocktail glass over fresh crushed ice.
Slowly pour pomegranate syrup down the side of the cocktail.

7. Tommy's Margarita

INGREDIENTS

2 ounces blanco tequila
1 ounce fresh lime juice
½ ounce agave nectar
Salt for rim

DIRECTIONS

Combine tequila, lime juice, and agave in a cocktail shaker.
Shake with ice until the shaker is slightly frosted over.
Strain over fresh ice in a salt-rimmed rocks glass.

8. Corpse Reviver

INGREDIENTS

DIRECTIONS

25ml gin
Half a lemon, juiced
25ml Cointreau
25ml sweet vermouth
A dash of absinthe

Combine all ingredients into a shaker and shake well with ice. Strain into a tall glass and garnish with lemon.

9. Aviation

INGREDIENTS

DIRECTIONS

25ml gin
A squeeze of lemon juice
10ml maraschino liqueur
Dash of crème de Violette
Blueberries (optional)

Shake up all the ingredients in a cocktail shaker with ice (except the blueberries), and strain into a cocktail glass. Garnish with blueberries.

10. Amaretto Sour

INGREDIENTS

50ml Amaretto
Half a lemon, juiced
Half an egg white
1 tsp cherry syrup
1 cherry

DIRECTIONS

Combine all the ingredients in a blender with a few ice cubes. Pour into a short glass and garnish with a cherry.

11. Gin Fizz

INGREDIENTS

DIRECTIONS

1 ¾ oz Gin
1 oz Lemon
3/4 oz Simple syrup
As needed Soda

Combine all ingredients in shaker tin, excluding soda. Add ice to small shaker tin. Shake vigorously, until tin is frosted over.
Strain into chilled highball glass with fresh ice and soda.
Garnish with lemon wedge and enjoy.

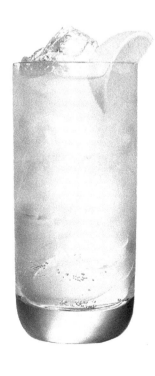

12. Caribbean Old Fashioned

INGREDIENTS

1 ounce white rum
1 ounce aged rum
½ ounce demerara syrup
3 dashes tropical bitters, such as Mister Bitters Sweet & Sour

DIRECTIONS

Combine all ingredients in a mixing glass with ice. Stir to chill and combine. Strain into a rocks glass over an ice sphere, or regular cubed ice.
Garnish & enjoy!

13. Americano

INGREDIENTS

DIRECTIONS

1 oz Campari
1 oz Sweet vermouth
2 oz Soda

Combine all ingredients in a rocks glass
Add ice.
Garnish with orange wedge and enjoy.

14. Vieux Carre

INGREDIENTS

1 ¼ oz Rye
1 ¼ oz Cognac
1 oz Sweet Vermouth
1 Bar spoon Benedictine
1 dash Angostura Bitters
1 dash Peychaud's Bitters

DIRECTIONS

Combine all ingredients in mixing glass with ice.
Stir.
Strain into chilled cocktail glass.
Garnish with lemon twist and enjoy..

15. Pisco Sour

INGREDIENTS

DIRECTIONS

2 oz Pisco
1 oz Lime
3/4 oz Gum Arabic syrup, can be substituted with Simple Syrup
1 egg white (optional)

Combine all ingredients in shaker tin.
Add a few chips of ice.
Shake until ice chips are dissolved.
Fill tin with ice.
Shake vigorously, until tin is frosted over.
Strain into chilled cocktail glass
Garnish with Angostura Bitters and enjoy.

16. Paloma

INGREDIENTS

DIRECTIONS

2 oz Reposado or Blanco tequila
1 oz Lime
1 each Pinch of salt
As needed Grapefruit soda

Combine ingredients in a highball.
Add ice.
Garnish with a grapefruit wheel and enjoy.

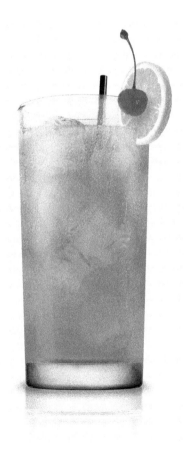

17. French 75

INGREDIENTS

DIRECTIONS

1 oz Gin
¾ oz Lemon
1 oz Simple Syrup
3 oz Champagne

Combine all ingredients in shaker tin, excluding Champagne.
Add ice to small shaker tin.
Shake vigorously, until tin is frosted over.
Strain into champagne flute with champagne.
Garnish with lemon twist and enjoy.

18. Sazerac

INGREDIENTS

DIRECTIONS

3 oz Rye or Brandy
1/2 oz Demerara syrup
10 dashes Peychaud's
Bitters
1 ea Lemon twist
As needed Absinthe

Combine all ingredients in mixing glass with ice.
Stir.
Strain into chilled rocks glass rinsed with absinthe, with no ice.
Garnish with lemon twist and enjoy.

18. Mai Tai

INGREDIENTS

2 ounces blended rum, such as Appleton Estate Reserve Blend or Denizen Merchant's Reserve
¾ ounce lime juice
¾ ounce orgeat syrup
½ ounce orange liqueur
Mint sprig

DIRECTIONS

Combine all ingredients, except mint, in a shaker.
Add crushed ice and shake vigorously, until shaker is frosted over.
Fill a double rocks glass with fresh crushed ice.
Strain cocktail into glass.
Garnish with mint sprig.

20. Harvey Wallbanger

INGREDIENTS

1 1/2 ounces vodka
4 ounces orange juice
1/2 ounce Galliano
L'Autentico
Orange slice, garnish
Maraschino cherry, garnish

DIRECTIONS

The Harvey Wallbanger is a fun and simple vodka cocktail that was created in the 1950s but really gained popularity during the disco era of the '70s. The recipe is very simple: mix a screwdriver and top it with a Galliano float. Galliano L'Autentico is a golden-colored sweet liqueur made with a blend of herbs, spices, and vanilla.

A Harvey Wallbanger is a fruity, sweet, and herbal mixture that's totally refreshing. It's also easy to mix up and a great way to practice a basic bartending skill.

21. Raffles Singapore Sling

INGREDIENTS

50ml gin
25ml lemon juice
25ml sugar syrup
125ml chilled soda water

DIRECTIONS
Put the gin, lemon juice, and sugar syrup in a tall glass, three-quarters filled with ice cubes, and top off with soda water. Stir, decorate the glass with a slice of lemon, and a stirrer.

22. Jungle Bird Recipe

INGREDIENTS

1 ½ ounces rum, Jamaican or blackstrap
¾ ounce Campari
½ ounce fresh lime juice
½ ounce simple syrup
1 ½ ounces pineapple juice

DIRECTIONS
Combine all ingredients in a cocktail shaker with ice, and shake to combine and chill. Pour into a rocks glass over fresh ice.

23. Cosmopolitan Recipe

INGREDIENTS

DIRECTIONS

1 1/2 oz Vodka
½ oz Cranberry juice
¾ oz Lime
¾ oz Cointreau L'unique

Combine all ingredients in shaker tin
Add ice.
Shake vigorously, until tin is frosted over.
Strain into chilled cocktail glass
Garnish with lime twist and enjoy.

24. Vodka Martini Recipe

INGREDIENTS

DIRECTIONS

2 ½ ounces vodka
½ ounce dry vermouth
Lemon twist

Combine vodka and vermouth in a mixing glass. Stir with ice until chilled. Strain into a chilled coupe or Martini glass. Gently express a lemon peel over the top of the drink, then garnish with the lemon zest.

25. Caipirinha Recipe

INGREDIENTS

DIRECTIONS

2 oz Cachaça
1 ea Whole lime, in wedges
2 tsp Extra fine white sugar

Combine all ingredients in rocks glass.
Muddle
Top with crushed ice.
Enjoy.

26. Tom Collins

INGREDIENTS

2 oz Gin
1 oz Lemon
1 oz Simple Syrup
As needed Soda

DIRECTIONS

Combine ingredients in a highball glass.
Add ice.
Garnish with lemon wheel and enjoy.

27. Boulevardier

INGREDIENTS

1 ½ oz Bourbon
1 oz Campari
1 oz Sweet Vermouth

DIRECTIONS

Combine all ingredients in mixing glass with ice.
Stir.
Strain into chilled rocks glass over fresh ice.
Garnish with an orange twist and enjoy.

28. Clover Club

INGREDIENTS

DIRECTIONS

1 ½ oz Gin
1 oz Lemon
1 oz Raspberry syrup
1 ea Egg white

Combine all ingredients in shaker tin.
Add a few chips of ice.
Shake until ice chips are dissolved.
Fill tin with ice.
Shake vigorously, until tin is frosted over.
Strain into chilled cocktail glass.
Enjoy.

29. Corpse Reviver

INGREDIENTS

DIRECTIONS

1 oz Gin

¾ oz Triple sec

¾ oz Lemon

¾ oz Lillet Blanc

As needed Absinthe

Combine all ingredients in shaker tin, excluding absinthe.

Ice small shaker tin.

Shake vigorously, until tin is frosted over.

Strain into chilled cocktail glass rinsed with absinthe.

Garnish with lemon twist and enjoy.

30. Penicillin

INGREDIENTS

2 ounces blended Scotch, such as Monkey Shoulder or Famous Grouse
¾ ounce fresh lemon juice
¾ ounce honey simple syrup
4 nickel-sized slices of ginger
¼ ounce smoky Islay Scotch

DIRECTIONS

Put ginger slices and honey syrup in the base of a shaker and gently muddle.
Combine other ingredients (except Islay Scotch) and shake with ice.
Double-strain into an ice-filled rocks glass.
Float the Islay Scotch over the top of the drink by pouring it over a bar spoon for even distribution.
Garnish with candied ginger on a cocktail pick.

31. Moscow Mule

INGREDIENTS

DIRECTIONS

2 ounces vodka
3 ounces ginger beer
Juice of half a lime, and
lime wedge for garnish

Add vodka, ginger beer, and lime juice to a copper mug (or highball glass).
Fill mug with crushed ice.
Stir well.
Garnish with lime wedge and enjoy.

32. Groovy Gimlet

INGREDIENTS

DIRECTIONS

2 ounces Butterfly Pea Tea
Gin
¾ ounce lime juice
¾ ounce toasted coconut
syrup

Combine all ingredients in a
cocktail shaker with ice
Shake for approximately 30
seconds to chill and
combine ingredients
Fine strain into a Nick &
Nora glass
Garnish with edible flower

33. Bloody Mary

INGREDIENTS

DIRECTIONS

2 oz Vodka

5 oz Tomato juice

1/2 oz Fresh lemon Juice

½ oz Worcestershire

Pinch Pepper

Pinch Celery salt

Combine all ingredients in a
Collins or highball glass.
Add ice.
Stir well.
Garnish with lemon, celery,
olives, and enjoy.

34. Mojito

INGREDIENTS

DIRECTIONS

2 oz White Rum
1 oz Lime
3/4 oz Simple Syrup
10 Mint leaves, and mint
sprig for garnish

Gently muddle mint leaves
in Collins or highball glass,
taking care not to break the
leaves.
Add remaining ingredients
to the glass.
Mix well.
Add crushed ice.
Garnish with mint sprig and
enjoy.

35. Aperol Spritz

INGREDIENTS

DIRECTIONS

2 ounces Aperol
3 ounces Prosecco
Club soda to top
Orange wedge or green
olive for garnish (optional)

Pour Aperol and Prosecco
into a wine glass filled with
ice.
Top with soda.
Stir gently to combine.
Add garnish, if using.

36. Manhattan

INGREDIENTS

2 ½ oz Rye
1 oz Sweet Vermouth
2 dashes Angostura

DIRECTIONS

Combine all ingredients in mixing glass with ice.
Stir.
Strain into chilled cocktail glass
Garnish with a cherry and enjoy.

37. Whiskey Sour

INGREDIENTS

2 ounces whiskey
(preferably bourbon)
1 ounce lemon juice
¾ ounce simple syrup
1 egg white
Garnish: brandied cherry,
Angostura bitters (to taste),
or lemon peel

DIRECTIONS

Add all ingredients to a
mixing tin and shake with
ice (wet shake) until
properly chilled.
Remove the ice and shake
again (dry shake) to
emulsify.
Double strain over ice into
a rocks glass and garnish as
you please.

38. Espresso Martini

INGREDIENTS

1 ounce vodka, preferably Belvedere Smógory Forest
¾ ounce coffee liqueur, preferably Mr. Black Cold Brew Coffee Liqueur
1 ¼ ounces fresh espresso
½ ounce simple syrup, (1:1, sugar:water)
Garnish: 3 coffee beans

DIRECTIONS

Combine all ingredients in a mixing tin and shake vigorously with ice.
Strain into a coupette glass.
Garnish with three coffee beans.

39. Margarita

INGREDIENTS

2 ounces mezcal
½ ounce Aperol
½ ounce fresh lime juice
½ ounce fresh lemon juice
¾ ounce strawberry-
rhubarb syrup (recipe
follows)
Pinch of sea salt
Fresh mint
Lime wheel and strawberry,
for garnish (optional)

DIRECTIONS

Add 4 or 5 large mint leaves
to the bottom of a cocktail
shaker tin, and gently
muddle with the strawberry-
rhubarb syrup.
Add the rest of the
ingredients, ice, and shake
to combine.
Double-strain into a rocks
glass over
fresh ice.
Garnish
with a
healthy of
sprig of mint,
lime wheel, and a
skewered strawberry.

40. Gin Martini

INGREDIENTS

DIRECTIONS

2 ¾ oz Gin
¾ oz Dry vermouth
Lemon twist or olives for garnish

Combine ingredients in an ice-filled mixing glass or shaker.
Stir vigorously for 15 seconds.
Strain into chilled coupe or Martini glass.
Garnish with lemon twist or olives and enjoy.

41. Daiquiri

INGREDIENTS

2 oz white rum
¾ oz lime juice
¾ oz simple syrup
Lime wedge

DIRECTIONS

Combine all ingredients, except lime wedge, in a shaker.
Add ice and shake vigorously, until tin is frosted over.
Strain cocktail into a chilled coupe glass.
Garnish with a lime wedge and enjoy.

42. Negroni

INGREDIENTS

1 ounce Calvados
1 ounce sweet vermouth
1 ounce red bitter

DIRECTIONS

Pour Calvados, sweet vermouth, and red bitter into a mixing glass with ice.
Stir ingredients.
Strain over fresh ice into rocks glass.
Garnish with orange twist.

43. Lynchburg Lemonade

INGREDIENTS

DIRECTIONS

1 1/2 ounces Tennessee
whiskey
1 ounce triple sec
1 ounce lemon juice
4 ounces lemon-lime soda

Gather the ingredients.
Pour the whiskey, triple sec,
and lemon juice into a
collins glass and add ice.
Top with soda.
Stir well and garnish with
lemon slices.
Serve and enjoy.

44. Scotch and Soda

INGREDIENTS

DIRECTIONS

2 ounces Scotch whisky
1 to 6 ounces club soda, to taste

Gather the ingredients.
In a highball or old-fashioned glass filled with ice, pour the Scotch.
Top with the club soda and stir well. Serve and enjoy.

45. Seven and Seven Mixed Drink

INGREDIENTS

DIRECTIONS

2 ounces Seagrams's 7
Crown Whiskey
4 to 6 ounces 7-Up soda, to
taste
Lemon wedge, garnish

Gather the ingredients.
Pour the whiskey into a
highball glass filled with ice.
Top with 7-Up.
Garnish with a lemon
wedge. Serve and enjoy.

46. Classic Whiskey Ginger

INGREDIENTS

DIRECTIONS

1 1/2 ounces Irish whiskey
5 ounces ginger ale
1 lime wedge

Gather the ingredients.

Pour the whiskey into a highball glass filled with ice.

Fill with ginger ale.

Squeeze a lime wedge over the drink and drop it in.

Stir.

Serve and enjoy.

47. Whiskey Highball

INGREDIENTS

DIRECTIONS

2 ounces whiskey
4 to 6 ounces ginger ale (or
club soda), to taste

Gather the ingredients.
Fill a highball glass with ice.
Pour the whiskey into the
glass.
Top with ginger ale. Serve
and enjoy.

48. Tequila Sunrise

INGREDIENTS

DIRECTIONS

2 ounces tequila

4 ounces orange juice

1/2 ounce grenadine

Orange slice, garnish

Maraschino cherry, garnish

Gather the ingredients.

In a highball glass filled with ice cubes, pour the tequila and orange juice. Stir well.

Slowly pour the grenadine around the inside edge of the glass. It will sink and gradually rise to mix with the other ingredients.

Garnish with an orange slice and cherry. Serve and enjoy.

49. Sidecar

INGREDIENTS

DIRECTIONS

60ml Cognac (or brandy)
30ml Cointreau
Half a lemon, juiced
1 orange wheel or lemon
twist and ice cubes to serve

Shake the Cognac, Cointreau and lemon juice with ice in a cocktail shaker. Strain and serve in a classic cocktail glass. Garnish with orange or lemon.

50. Vesper

INGREDIENTS

DIRECTIONS

30ml gin
10ml vodka
5ml Lillet Blanc
Lemon garnish

Shake all ingredients in a shaker with ice, strain into a chilled martini glass. Garnish with lemon.

51. Pornstar Martini

INGREDIENTS

30ml vanilla vodka
15ml Pessoa
1 ripe passionfruit
1 squeeze lime juice
1 tsp sugar syrup
75ml Prosecco

DIRECTIONS

Add the passionfruit pulp and all other ingredients into a shaker with ice, shake well and strain into a martini glass. Top up with Prosecco.

52. Cosmopolitan

INGREDIENTS

DIRECTIONS

50ml gin
1 lemon, juiced
1 tbsp honey

Pour all ingredients into a shaker.
Shake well and strain into a cocktail glass.
Garnish with a lemon slice.

53. White Lady

INGREDIENTS

DIRECTIONS

50ml gin
25ml Cointreau
20ml fresh lemon juice
15ml sugar syrup
Egg white

Add all ingredients into a cocktail shaker and shake well. Add a few ice cubes and shake again.
Strain into a (martini) glass.

54. Bamboo

INGREDIENTS

40ml sherry
20ml sweet vermouth
10ml dry vermouth
2 dashes Angostura bitters

DIRECTIONS

Stir all ingredients together and strain into a Martini glass. Garnish with an orange twist.

55. Ramos Gin Fizz

INGREDIENTS

DIRECTIONS

35ml gin
1 tbsp triple sec
2 tsp orange flower water
25ml freshly squeezed lemon juice
2 tsp sugar syrup
25ml egg white
25ml double cream
soda water, to serve

Pour all the ingredients aside from the soda water into a cocktail shaker and shake well.
Strain into a highball glass then top up with the soda.

56. Old Cuban

INGREDIENTS

70ml dark rum
40g caster sugar
Half a lime, juiced
A sprig of fresh mint
Dash of Angostura bitters
50ml Prosecco

DIRECTIONS

Mix sugar with 25ml warm water to make a syrup. Then, add the syrup, lime juice and rum into a shaker. Add the mint, Angostura and some ice cubes and shake well. Strain into a chilled cocktail glass and top up with Prosecco.

57. Blood and Sand

INGREDIENTS

20ml sweet vermouth
20ml Scotch whiskey
20ml blood orange juice
20ml cherry liqueur

DIRECTIONS

Add all the ingredients into a cocktail shaker and shake well with ice. Strain into a cocktail glass and garnish with an orange slice.

58. Paloma

INGREDIENTS

DIRECTIONS

50ml tequila
10ml lime juice
60ml pink grapefruit juice
Soda water

Dip the rim of a highball glass in water, shake off any excess, and press into salt to coat. Add all the ingredients minus the soda water into a cocktail shaker with ice, and shake well. Strain into a chilled glass and top with soda water.

59. Death in the Afternoon

INGREDIENTS

DIRECTIONS

10ml absinthe
135ml Champagne

Add absinthe to a
Champagne flute, then top
up with Champagne.

60. Passionfruit Martini Mocktail

INGREDIENTS

DIRECTIONS

1 passionfruit
Half a lemon, juiced
1 egg white
50ml alcohol-free spirit
2 tsp sugar syrup
Sparkling grape juice

Scoop the passionfruit flesh into a cocktail shaker and add all ingredients except the sparkling grape juice. Shake until frothy. Add a handful of ice and shake again vigorously. Double strain into chilled martini glasses.

61. Virgin Paloma

INGREDIENTS

DIRECTIONS

1.5 limes, juiced
30ml grapefruit juice
30ml agave syrup
Pinch of sea salt

Combine all ingredients into a cocktail shaker and shake well with ice. Strain over ice and serve in a tall glass.

62. Dark 'n' Stormy

INGREDIENTS

DIRECTIONS

50ml dark rum

Half a lime, juiced

Build the cocktail over ice in

2 dashes of Angostura
bitters

a highball glass. Garnish
with a lime wedge.

100ml ginger beer

63. Gimlet

INGREDIENTS

DIRECTIONS

50ml gin
50ml Rose's lime juice
Slice of lime (optional)

Add the gin and lime juice into a mixing jug with ice and stir until very cold. Strain the mixture into a chilled glass and garnish with lime.

64. Boulevardier

INGREDIENTS

DIRECTIONS

35ml bourbon whisky
30ml sweet red vermouth
30ml Campari

Shake all ingredients in a cocktail shaker with ice and strain into a short glass.

65. Southside

INGREDIENTS

DIRECTIONS

60ml gin
8 mint leaves
1 lime, juiced
15ml sugar syrup
Soda water or Champagne
(optional)

Add all ingredients to a shaker with ice and shake well. Strain and pour into a tall glass over more ice. Top up with soda or Champagne for the variations.

66. Last Word

INGREDIENTS

DIRECTIONS

30ml dry gin
20ml Green Chartreuse liqueur
20ml maraschino liqueur
Half a lime, juiced
10ml chilled water

Shake all ingredients with ice and strain into a chilled 'Coupe' glass.

67. Bramble

INGREDIENTS

50ml gin
Half a lemon, juiced
A dash of sugar syrup
1 tsp of crème de mure

DIRECTIONS

Add gin, lemon juice and sugar syrup to a cocktail shaker and shake well with ice. Strain into a short glass over crushed ice. Drizzle the crème de mure so it 'bleeds' into the drink.

Lightning Source UK Ltd.
Milton Keynes UK
UKHW020718030622
403936UK00001B/3